THE BEATLES

YEAH! YEAH! YEAH!

MICK MANNING • BRITA GRANSTRÖM

F

FRANCES LINCOLN
CHILDREN'S BOOKS

TWIST AND SHOUT

In Liverpool, a busy city in war-torn Britain, a baby is twisting and shouting in his pram to the sound of air-raid sirens. This baby's name is John Winston Lennon and one day his *Twist and Shout* will rock the world – but not just yet. By the time the war ends, in 1945, John is living with his aunty Mimi and her husband, George. He's started school and even has his own gang. One day, when Mimi goes to meet him, she sees boys fighting. . . . She's horrified to recognise that one of them is John! "I was *Just William* really," says John Lennon years later.

THIS WAY TO THE AIR RAID SHEL

John Winston Lennon

He's a lovely little chap, Julia!

John Winston Lennon!

John was only four when his mum, Julia, and his dad, Fred, split up. Julia's sister, Mimi, had loved John from the moment she first saw him; so when Julia began building a new life with a new partner, Mimi often looked after John at her house in a leafy suburb of Liverpool. Over time, this arrangement became permanent, and John moved in with Mimi and her husband, George.

John loved reading: from *Just William* adventures and *The Wind in the Willows* to the dream-like world of *Alice in Wonderland* and the nonsense limericks of Edward Lear.

"This boy shows real talent!"

THE HARMONICA

What's that wailing sound? It's John! He's on his way to Scotland to visit his cousin Stanley in Edinburgh, and he has been playing his battered old harmonica all the way from Liverpool. He's showing real talent; yet he's been blowing that harmonica for mile after mile and it's starting to drive some passengers crazy! But the driver likes it – he likes it so much that he promises to give John a much better harmonica when they get to Edinburgh.

John's mum, Julia, had found a new partner and had a new family, but she still visited John when she could.

Keep up the good work, kid!

Thanks, mister!

The next morning, at the bus depot, the driver showed John a professional 'chromatic' harmonica that he'd found on a bus. It had never been claimed, so the kindly man gave it to John. Many years later, John's harmonica-playing helped to give The Beatles' first single, *Love Me Do*, its distinctive sound.

QUARRY BANK HIGH SCHOOL

John is easily bored at school. He feels his teachers at Quarry Bank don't encourage his interest in Art, so he spends most of his time mucking about in class. He styles his hair like his rebel-hero, Elvis, and he's turned a school exercise book into a comic he calls *The Daily Howl*. It makes his mates giggle, but in his school report his teacher writes:

'Certainly on the road to failure... hopeless... rather a clown in class ... wasting other pupils' time.'

Before the 1950s, teenagers had always dressed like their parents... there were no special fashions for young people. But Rock 'n' Roll music changed all that. Fans became known as Rockers and Teddy Boys.

American Rock 'n' Roll singers such as Elvis Presley and Little Richard were taking the world by storm. Meanwhile Scottish star Lonnie Donegan had begun a craze for 'Skiffle' – a style of banjo music using home-made instruments such as washboards and pans.

The guitar's all very well, John, but you'll never make a living out of it!

When John was 16, with the help of his mum, he got a cheap acoustic guitar by mail-order, called a *Gallotone Champion*. Julia taught him some banjo-style chords, and he soon formed a Skiffle group with schoolmates. He called them The Quarrymen, and it was a new kind of gang for John.

PAUL MCCARTNEY

This is Paul, and he was born in 1942. His mother, Mary, is a midwife and his dad, Jim, is a salesman who used to have his own jazz band before the war. Jim still thumps out a good tune on the piano and he's fixed up some earphones so that Paul can lie on his bed and listen to the radio. Paul listens to Rock 'n' Roll, comedy shows and documentaries. He remembers the facts as well as the tunes, using them in his essays for school. It's what got him into the best school in the area: The Liverpool Institute.

At the age of 14, Paul swapped a trumpet his dad had bought him for a *Zenith Model 17* guitar. At first he couldn't make it work! It just jangled and twanged. Paul couldn't understand it... what was he doing wrong? Suddenly he realised – it was strung for a right-handed player, and he was left-handed! He got it restrung and started practising....

Because Paul was at the Grammar school he was teased by some of the local kids and called a 'college pudding'.

But on the bus he palled up with another Liverpool Institute pupil, a younger lad called George Harrison. They shared an interest... Rock 'n' Roll!

In 1956 Paul was devastated by the sudden death of his mum from breast cancer. He was only 14 and from then on he and his brother, Michael, were looked after by their dad.

Paul and John hit it off and within weeks
Paul had joined John's band.

THE QUARRYMEN

John's schoolboy band, The Quarrymen, play wherever they can.
They sing hits by stars such as Lonnie Donegan and Elvis Presley,
and already have a reputation as the local Teddy Boys.
Today they are playing at St Peter's Church fête, not far from
John's home, and something special is going to happen: something
that will, one day, rock the world. A mutual friend, Ivan Vaughan,
is going to introduce Paul to John. Paul is already impressed
with John's tough-guy image and later, when Paul plays and sings
for him, John is knocked out!

One day, while practising together, Paul sang John some songs he had written himself.
John was amazed. He'd never thought about writing songs. . . it was even more fun
than writing *The Daily Howl*. From that moment they began writing songs together
and scribbled 'A Lennon-McCartney Original' on each one.

1958

GEORGE HARRISON

Do you remember Paul's friend on the school bus, George Harrison? Well, George is turning into a great guitarist, and one day Paul brings him along to meet John and audition for the band. At first John thinks George is too young because he's only 15. But later, Paul arranges for George to play guitar again for John, this time on the top deck of a Liverpool bus. George plays so well that John changes his mind. Now, with three guitars, the Quarrymen are less of a Skiffle group – and more of a Rock 'n' Roll group.

John was a rebel, but he still got changed into his rocker's jeans at the bus stop so he wouldn't upset his aunty Mimi. The new Beat music, named after its toe-tapping beat, was the birth of modern pop music.

George was born in 1943. He went to the same primary school as John but was in a younger class. George liked to sit at the back of the class and draw guitars. When he was little, his mum loved to tune in to Indian music on the radio. This music would influence George for the rest of his life.

In 1958 John's mum, Julia, was killed while crossing the road on her way home from visiting Mimi. John was devastated.

Coffee-bar clubs with live music were the places teenagers met up. It was a great chance for up-and-coming Beat groups to play live.

JOHNNY AND THE MOONDOGS

John is at Liverpool Art School now, and his Quarry Bank schoolmates have all left the band. When flat-mate Stuart Sutcliffe joins John, Paul and George, they call themselves Johnny and The Moondogs. But Stu suggests changing the band's name again. They try different names: The Beatals, The Silver Beats, The Beetles. Then, one night in John's student flat, a poet friend encourages them to spell their name with an 'a'… to show they play Beat music. The Beatles get so carried away that they forget about a chicken pie in the oven and it catches fire!

The Casbah Club was a small club in the cellar of Mona Best's house. Mona had first let the boys play there as the Quarrymen on the club's opening night. They soon befriended Mona's teenage son, Pete, and even helped decorate. When, in 1960, another coffee-bar owner offered the boys full-time work playing in German nightclubs, they couldn't believe their luck. But they needed a drummer. Then they remembered Pete played drums....

HAMBURG

When The Beatles arrive in Germany, they find the Hamburg nightclubs are not at all like the Liverpool coffee-bar scene. They are open all hours, and full of sailors and rockers who are more interested in fighting than listening. So they get the crowds' attention by dressing in leather and doing crazy things: screaming into their microphones, telling jokes and stomping their feet. The toughs stop fighting and begin to watch the 'crazy English guys'. The Beatles are beginning to learn the art of showmanship! John later says: "I may have been born in Liverpool, but I grew up in Hamburg."

At one club, The Beatles split the 12-hour shift with another Liverpool act called Rory Storm and the Hurricanes. The Hurricanes' drummer often stayed behind to watch The Beatles. They soon made friends. He shared their dead-pan humour and they liked his cool name: Ringo Starr…

They look like they're having fun!

Paul invited Pete Best to join them on drums. Although Pete was quite shy, he was a good drummer. When they drove off the ferry in Hamburg, they found the clubs were in the roughest part of town. They had to play for up to 12 hours at a time with only short breaks in between… but they loved it!

BUNK BEDS

In Hamburg, The Beatles are shocked to find their home is a walk-in store cupboard. When they open the door they don't see any furniture, just bunk beds. It's next door to the Ladies toilet. Yuck! With no bath or shower, they have to wash in the toilet sink. But John makes a good group leader: whenever his band gets down in the dumps, he encourages them by shouting, "Where are we going, boys?" And the others shout back, "To the toppermost of the poppermost, Johnny!"

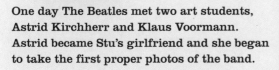

One day The Beatles met two art students, Astrid Kirchherr and Klaus Voormann. Astrid became Stu's girlfriend and she began to take the first proper photos of the band.

What will the others think, Astrid?

They will love it, Stu!

One day she cut Stu's hair in a style poplar with German students. She also made a collarless modern jacket for him.

Ha-Ha!

That haircut looks like a mop!

At first John and Paul teased Stu for his haircut and for not wearing his leather rocker gear. But then one day, while on holiday together in Paris, John and Paul changed their hairstyles too. This was the haircut that they later made famous as the 'mop-top'. After a fall-out with the German club owner, The Beatles returned to Liverpool. But Stu decided to stay behind with Astrid and he left the band to study art.

THE CAVERN AND BRIAN EPSTEIN

Back home in Liverpool, The Beatles are soon playing in a popular club called The Cavern. Meanwhile, in a local record shop, customers have been asking the owner, Brian Epstein, about them. When Brian checks with his staff, they say that not only do The Beatles sometimes 'hang out' in his shop, he once actually kicked them out for not buying anything! Brian is curious and when he goes to The Cavern he sees 'raw talent'. He suggests that he should become their manager and The Beatles soon agree.

There was no digital music, or CDs, back then: only records made of a sort of plastic. The music came from a spiral groove in the record's surface that was picked up electronically by a needle called a 'stylus'. Mass-produced, affordable radios and record players encouraged teenagers to listen to and collect 'singles'. The Beatles appealed to this new, fast-growing market.

Record shops like Brian's sold 'singles' (records with one song on the A side and another on the B side, which lasted about three minutes). There were also EPs (extended singles with two songs on each side) and LPs ('long players' or 'albums', which were larger and had around five or six songs on each side). Records often had well designed cardboard sleeves displaying photos of the group.

Brian got the boys to record a demo-tape and played it to many London record companies – but nobody seemed interested. They even had an audition for one company, but were turned down.

GOODBYE PETE, HELLO RINGO

One day Brian meets a record producer called George Martin. George gives these Liverpool lads an audition and likes what he hears. At last they get a record deal! Meanwhile, The Beatles have taken Brian's advice and changed their image. They now wear suits – and John, Paul and George have mop-top haircuts! But things don't go well for Pete Best, and their old buddy Ringo replaces him on drums. Their first single, *Love Me Do*, shoots into the charts. After they record their next single, *Please Please Me*, George Martin says, "You've just recorded your first Number One, boys!" His prediction comes true.

If there is anything you're not happy with, boys, just let me know.

These boys are cheeky, but I like them!

I'm sorry, Pete, you're fired.

The Beatles had already begun to feel that they didn't have much in common with Pete; his personality was different from theirs, he was quieter and he didn't always share their jokes. So despite Pete's popularity with the fans, when George Martin announced he wasn't happy with Pete's drumming on The Beatles' debut recordings, the band decided to fire him. When Brian Epstein broke the news, it was a terrible shock for Pete.

We want you in the band, Ringo!

Fantastic!

Ringo was working in a holiday camp when he got the call. He happily swapped his Teddy Boy's quiff for a Beatle mop-top. At first Pete Best's fans chanted, "Pete forever, Ringo never!" One fan even gave George a black eye. But they soon accepted Ringo as a Beatle.

More hits followed. On The Beatles' first LP, also called *Please Please Me*, they recorded their version of *Twist and Shout*. John had a sore throat which produced such a raunchy sound that it is still considered the ultimate British Rock 'n' Roll vocal. Fans began to follow them everywhere, and the boys had to run to escape being torn into souvenir-sized pieces. When John married his girlfriend Cynthia, they tried to keep it a secret.

In 1963, The Beatles were invited to play at the Royal Command Performance in front of the Queen. They won 15 million TV viewers' hearts when John made a cheeky joke: "For the people in the cheaper seats, clap your hands... and the rest of you, if you'll just rattle your jewellery."

When fans begged for souvenirs at the door, Mimi gave away John's old shirt buttons, and Ringo's mum, Elsie, even gave away Ringo's old socks!

BEATLEMANIA

Brian is turning The Beatles into something unique; whatever they sing, whatever they say, now appeals to millions of faithful fans. The press names this phenomenon Beatlemania, but it is being earned with hard work. In 1963 alone, The Beatles play over 230 concerts across the UK and Sweden. Wherever they perform it is chaos: fans scream so loud they drown out the music, and because George once admitted to liking Jelly Babies, fans bombard the stage with jelly sweets! With the release of their second LP, *With The Beatles*, they get the nickname 'The Fab Four'. But Brian wonders why The Beatles' records are flopping in the USA. In fact no UK pop stars have made it big over there… if only John and Paul could come up with the right song.

John and Paul worked closely together when composing new songs. John once described it as 'one on one, eyeball to eyeball' and one day, when Paul hit a chord, John's eyes lit up. The result was a new single, *I Want To Hold Your Hand*.

I Want To Hold Your Hand

The Americans don't just like the new single – they go crazy for it! *I Want To Hold Your Hand* sells five million copies in the USA alone and tops the US charts for seven weeks. On 9th February, 1964, when The Beatles appear on US TV on the hugely popular Ed Sullivan Show, they attract 73 million viewers – the largest audience ever recorded. Crime rates drop to an all-time low, as even criminals stay home to watch the show! At last, all The Beatles' previous records start to sell like hot cakes in America as Beatlemania takes the USA by storm. Englishmen haven't caused such hysteria in America since Charles Dickens visited, 120 years earlier!

Hello, America!

I Want to Hold Your Hand!

Wow, we're on U.S. telly!

TV appearances were the ideal way for pop groups to promote themselves. Brian Epstein saw the potential of TV and soon realised that the cheeky 'fab four' charmed everyone while on camera.

The Beatles' first visit to the USA in February, 1964, was only 11 weeks after the assassination of President J F Kennedy in Dallas. America was still in shock. When they returned to tour the USA in August, they met some of their own musical heroes, including Bob Dylan. Later, in 1965, they visited Elvis Presley.

The Beatles' appearances on US TV made British groups fashionable with American teenagers, and an 'invasion' of exciting new British groups soon began: The Rolling Stones, The Kinks, The Moody Blues, The Animals....

I have a dream...

In 1965, in tune with the civil rights protests for racial equality in the USA, led by figures such as Martin Luther King, The Beatles refused to play a show in Florida unless they were assured the audience would not be racially segregated.

Also in 1965, American combat troops joined the Vietnam war, and over the next ten years 58,000 young Americans were killed in Vietnam – more young people than filled Shea Stadium.

WOW!

There's around 56,000 people in the stadium today!

...and they are all screaming!

TOURING THE USA

Brian had signed a movie contract, back in 1963, for The Beatles to make some musical comedies. After the release of the first film, *A Hard Day's Night*, in 1964, excitement cranked up to fever pitch ahead of their first month-long, sell-out US tour. Now, a year later, The Beatles return to tour the USA again; and here, at Shea Stadium in New York, they are playing to almost 56,000 fans. It's a record-breaking audience and the first ever stadium rock concert. Meanwhile, Beatles merchandise is selling like hot cakes worldwide: from singles and LPs to dresses, bubble-gum cards and even real samples of hair.

Later, in 1966, during their last US tour, John commented in an interview that The Beatles were 'more popular than Jesus'. This caused an uproar. Some concerts were cancelled. Protests and even death threats followed until John said sorry on TV.

A HARD DAY'S NIGHT

Made in 1964, this film plays on the idea of the band being on a hamster wheel of travelling and performing.

The lyrics talk of working hard and feeling exhausted, yet going home to a loved one, which makes everything all right again.

It's a song that working adults can relate to, especially those on night shift, from factory and postal workers to nurses and hospital porters.

HELP!

This film was made in 1965 as a sort of spoof on the James Bond movies. A priestess of a mysterious cult wants a ring that is stuck on Ringo's finger... whoever wears the ring must be sacrificed!

Lots of funny, zany things happen as the gang and a mad scientist chase the Beatles.

It was filmed in glamorous locations around the world and was a huge success.

Cinemas were packed with teenage fans!

FILM STARS

The Beatles' cheeky stage personalities are great on camera. Their first feature film, *A Hard Day's Night*, already a monster hit, has been nominated for two Oscars. Now their latest film, *Help!*, filmed in exotic locations across the world, is also a huge success. Since then George has been experimenting with an Indian stringed instrument called a sitar, which he picked up on the film set. He has always liked Indian music, ever since his mum listened to it on the radio. The sitar is such a beautiful instrument that George has fallen in love with it. In fact, he has decided to have sitar lessons with an expert....

Very good, George, very good indeed!

George began sitar lessons with Indian musician, Ravi Shankar. George's sitar playing can be heard on later Beatles songs such as *Norwegian Wood* and *Love You To*. His sitar playing influenced later songs by other groups such as: The Rolling Stones' *Paint it Black* and Traffic's *Hole in My Shoe*.

PAUL'S DREAM

One morning Paul wakes up with a beautiful tune in his head. For days he thinks it must be a classical piece he's heard… but slowly he realises the truth: he's composed it in his sleep! He begins trying to fit words to his tune. He even thinks up some lyrics that rhyme 'scrambled eggs' and 'love your legs'… but it's months before the right words come to him. During a long journey to stay with friends in Portugal, Paul finally writes the words to what will become one of the most famous songs ever written: *Yesterday*.

By the mid 1960s, Britain had became a world leader of the social revolution later known as the Swinging Sixties. This was thanks to the pop explosion led by The Beatles, not to mention British film-makers, photographers, writers, artists, the black and white optical patterns of 'Op Art', and fashion designers such as Mary Quant.

In October, 1965, John, Paul, George and Ringo were awarded MBE medals at Buckingham Palace. When Queen Elizabeth II asked them how long they had been together, Paul and Ringo jokily quoted the famous Victorian musical hall song, *My Old Dutch*. It is said that Her Majesty chuckled.

The Beatles secretly stayed in the seaside town of Berwick upon Tweed before beginning their last ever UK tour in Glasgow. On the way, a lorry driver flagged them down to tell them something had fallen off their roof. It was George's best guitar! By the time they found it in the dark it had been smashed to bits by the motorway traffic.

YESTERDAY

The words to this story of a broken love affair finally came to Paul in the back of a chauffeur-driven car, as he travelled to a friend's villa in Portugal in May 1965.

I have got this tune in my head.

At last, I've thought of the right words!

Paul couldn't wait to perform the song. When he arrived he rushed indoors for a guitar.

Well, what do you think?

Yesterday has since been recorded by over 1,600 artists and was voted the best song of the 20th Century in a BBC radio poll in 1999.

REVOLVER

Exhausted by years of almost non-stop touring, recording and film work, the band take a three-month break to develop new songs for their next album, *Revolver*. Paul comes up with a playful and catchy song he calls *Yellow Submarine*. Everyone loves it, and it is chosen as the next single alongside a serious but very beautiful song about loneliness, called *Eleanor Rigby*. Both songs become very famous, but *Yellow Submarine*, with Ringo's deadpan vocals, is the sing-along smash hit of 1966, played on the radio, whistled on buses and chanted in school playgrounds.

It's like a children's song!

ELEANOR RIGBY

Paul had a gift for telling stories about everyday people. Here he imagines two lonely people: a woman called Eleanor and a priest called Father Mackenzie. The beautiful tune's lyrics remind us about the tragedy of loneliness.

Lonely images include Eleanor picking up someone else's wedding confetti, the priest darning his own socks at night and finally the priest burying poor Eleanor. Instead of drums and guitars, a sensitive string quartet makes this an unforgettable song.

Paul thought he had made Eleanor up, but many years later a gravestone with the name Eleanor Rigby was discovered in the churchyard where John and Paul first met in 1957.

What's your name, baby?

You can't park here, sir!

One day, outside Abbey Road studios, Paul got a penalty ticket from a female traffic warden. Female traffic wardens had only recently started working in Britain, and the incident amused Paul. It inspired him to write a catchy song about falling in love with a traffic warden. 'Lovely Rita' appeared on the Beatles' next album…

Yeah, perfect!

YELLOW SUBMARINE

Inspired by Paul's childhood in the port of Liverpool, this song describes meeting a man who has sailed the seas in submarines, perhaps in World War Two.

In a time of anti-war protests, the irresistible chorus seemed to poke fun at military power.

It topped the UK charts in 1966 and inspired the animated musical film *Yellow Submarine* in 1968. Children's toys and posters followed.

1967

SGT PEPPER

The Beatles' next album, *Sgt Pepper's Lonely Hearts Club Band*, amazes everyone with beautiful songs, experimental music, military costumes and an unforgettable cover by the Pop artist Peter Blake. *Sgt Pepper*'s influence changes pop music forever and it is soon called the greatest record of all time. In the same year, John has his Rolls-Royce painted by gypsy caravan artists in a flower-power 'hippy' design....

John's discovery of a Victorian circus poster inspired his song, *Being For The Benefit of Mr. Kite!* As with many songs on *Sgt Pepper*, it used experimental music techniques: fairground sounds as well as tape recordings cut up and stuck back together. It became one of the most complex recordings on this influential album.

One day, John's son Julian brings home from school a painting of his friend Lucy, and she is in the sky with diamonds. John is knocked out! A song begins to grow in his imagination....

LUCY IN THE SKY WITH DIAMONDS

Inspired by his son's drawing and his own love of Edward Lear's verse and Lewis Caroll's books, John composed an imaginative song, celebrating the spirit of the Sixties.

...of a daydream-world. He ends by imagining a girl with eyes like kaleidoscopes. John's poetic lyrics, melody and vocals make it one of the most influential songs ever written.

Alice is drifting in a boat in a strange psychedelic landscape. John's lyrics conjure up amazing images...

STRAWBERRY FIELDS FOREVER

This song is about the power of happy memories and favourite places.

John is happily remembering the grounds of a children's home called Strawberry Field. Mimi took him to garden parties there.

He also used to sneak in and play there with his mates. In the song he says that when life gets hard he likes to imagine Strawberry Field.

Modern therapy techniques urge us all to visit a safe place in our heads when we are somewhere worrying or unpleasant – at the dentist for example.

ALL YOU NEED IS LOVE

After *Sgt Pepper*, The Beatles are invited to make the first ever live worldwide TV broadcast. They record *All You Need is Love*, a message of world peace and goodwill. John's fascination with the power of TV commercials and propaganda inspires a hypnotic chant of the word 'Love', while he sings to over 400 million global viewers that love is all that matters. It has a huge impact on a world scarred by the war still raging in Vietnam and reaches Number One in many countries, topping their previous double single, *Penny Lane* and *Strawberry Fields Forever*.

PENNY LANE

In the early sixties, while waiting to meet John at the bus station in Liverpool, Paul had jotted down some ideas. Now he turned it it into a nostalgic song full of everyday characters:

The barber and his shop-window photographs of hairstyles…

The banker without a coat in the pouring rain…

The pretty nurse selling poppies on the street for charity…

In September, 1967, inspired by Paul's home-movie experiments, the band made a musical comedy, *Magical Mystery Tour*, about a brightly coloured wizards' coach trip. But in the UK, colour TV technology was so new that the film was first screened in black and white leaving many people bemused; it became The Beatles' first critical failure. But it had some great new songs. In *I Am The Walrus*. John mischievously wove into the crazy lyrics a version of the old schoolboy rhyme about custard and dead dogs' eyes, as well as a radio extract from Shakespeare's *King Lear*.

APPLE RECORDS

In the summer of 1967 The Beatles' manager and friend, Brian Epstein, dies suddenly. The Beatles are stunned and shocked. But life goes on....
By December they have opened their own boutique in London and their own record label, Apple Records. In February, 1968, they visit a mystical Indian Guru, the Maharishi Mahesh Yogi, at his retreat in the Himalayas. Here they write lots of new songs, many of which will appear on their next LP, officially called *The Beatles*, but known as *The White Album*. However, things don't stay relaxed for long....

LADY MADONNA

In tune with the politics of womens' equality known in the 1960s as 'Women's Lib', and perhaps thinking of their own mothers, John and Paul wrote a homage to motherhood. They ask how everyday mothers across the world manage to make ends meet, raise a family and pay the rent.

Witty lyrics to a boogie-woogie piano sound take us through the days of the week: Tuesday's work never seems to end, Thursday night is spent darning stockings, Sunday creeps like a nun. Paul and John were making a light-hearted political point – every mother should be seen as a saint.

Love and Peace!

In India, out of the public eye, away from fanatical fans and nosy journalists, The Beatles studied meditation techniques and the Yogi's philosophy of peace and love. Somehow they had to carry on without the management skills of Brian Epstein.

OB-LA-DI OB-LA-DA

This popular sing-along song has a Reggae beat and was written at a time when Jamaican Reggae music was becoming popular in Britain and Europe.

It's a lighthearted and catchy love song, celebrating life. In fact, "Ob-La-Di-Ob-La-Da, life goes on, bra" was a phrase used by Jimmy Scott, a Nigerian friend of Paul's.

Desmond owns a market barrow.

Molly is a local singer.

A beautiful place, where beautiful people...

...Can buy beautiful things!

In 1969, George walked out after rows with the other members of the band. He wanted more of his songs on the albums. But he was persuaded to rejoin, and his composition *Here Comes the Sun*, with its melodic tune and hopeful lyrics, became one of The Beatles' most famous songs. He was not the first to walk out. Ringo had quit and rejoined a few months earlier....

OCTOPUS'S GARDEN

Fed up with the arguments that had begun while recording *The White Album*, Ringo quit the band and went on holiday.

I'm out of here!

It's "octopus" for lunch!

Over lunch, the captain of his yacht explained how octopuses collect shells and make 'gardens' under the sea...

Ringo was inspired to write a charming, lighthearted song.

Welcome back, Ringo!

When he decided to rejoin the band he found that John, Paul and George had filled the studio with thousands of flowers to welcome him back.

DRIFTING APART

John, Paul, George and Ringo are drifting in different directions – it's been happening for a while. They are spending more and more time away from the band, with their partners, families and friends. To try to get back to their roots, they film and record a live concert on the roof of their own record label headquarters. They record some great songs, but because they are unable to agree on how the final record should sound, the project is shelved. This will eventually become part of the *Let It Be* album and film.

This will make a great album cover.

While the *Let It Be* project was on hold, The Beatles recorded what became their final album, *Abbey Road*. With its iconic cover photograph of a zebra crossing, it is full of fabulous songs, but it is also clear that these songs, although original and exciting, are now mainly solo songs made by four individuals rather than a band.

NEW BEGINNINGS

Finally, in 1970, John, Paul, George and Ringo split up. They want to do their own things as solo artists. The Beatles have been the soundtrack to the 1960s, changing music forever and influencing the whole world with their messages of humanity and peace. Many musicians today continue to record Beatles songs. From Boy-bands to Punk rockers and Rap singers, you could say it all began with those fresh-faced, cheeky lads from Liverpool.

PAUL

Paul McCartney and his wife, Linda, formed a band called Wings. Their hits included the James Bond theme tune *Live and Let Die* and the record-breaking hit single, *Mull of Kintyre*, featuring a bagpipe band. Together with Mark Featherstone-Witty, Paul turned his and George's derelict old school into the Liverpool Institute for Performing Arts. It opened in 1996 and is now one of the UK's leading institutions for the performing arts. Paul McCartney was knighted in 1997, and his childhood home, 20 Forthlin Road in Liverpool, is now a museum owned by The National Trust.

JOHN

John Lennon and his second wife Yoko Ono set up The Plastic Ono Band. They collaborated with a group of musicians that included, occasionally, George and Ringo. John and Yoko had some huge hits with messages of peace and love: *Imagine*, *Power to the People*, *Happy Xmas (War is Over)*, and of course, *Give Peace a Chance* – a plea for world peace with the power of a sports stadium chant! Tragically, John Lennon was murdered by a deranged gunman in New York in 1980. Lennon's childhood home, Mendips, in Liverpool is now a museum owned by The National Trust.

RINGO

Ringo Starr acted in films and also collaborated with John, Paul and George on solo projects. They helped him to compose several hit records. In the 1980s Ringo formed The All Starr Band, an ever-changing group of famous musicians. His droll Liverpudlian accent can also be heard on the children's TV show, *Thomas the Tank Engine*.

GEORGE

George Harrison was a life-long admirer of Indian culture and spirituality, particularly Hinduism. He wrote many hits, including *My Sweet Lord*. George was also an executive producer with Hand-Made Films, producing movies such as *The Life of Brian* and *Withnail and I*. After a courageous battle with cancer, George died in 2001.

THE 1960s

The Beatles' music became the soundtrack to the amazing things that happened during the remarkable decade that was the 1960s. Many of those changes still affect our lives today. Here are just a few of them…

John F Kennedy is elected as president of the USA.

Yuri Gagarin is the first man in outer-space. It is the start of the 'space race' between the USA and Soviet Union. President Kennedy promises the USA 'a man on the moon' by the end of the decade.

The first trans-atlantic satellite is broadcast by Telstar.

The first ever computer video game is launched – *Spacewar!*

President Kennedy is assassinated in Dallas, Texas in November.

The first home video recording tape cassettes are produced.

Civil rights protests continue across the USA, led by Martin Luther King.

American combat troops join the Vietnam War.

1960

1961

1962

1963

1964

1965

The Beatles go on their first tour – to Hamburg.

The band are talent-spotted by Brian Epstein.

Ringo Starr joins the band.

Beatlemania begins.

The Beatles' first visit to the USA and appearances on US TV.

The Beatles perform the first ever stadium rock concert in history at She Stadium, New York City.